3/95

HUNGARY

...in Pictures

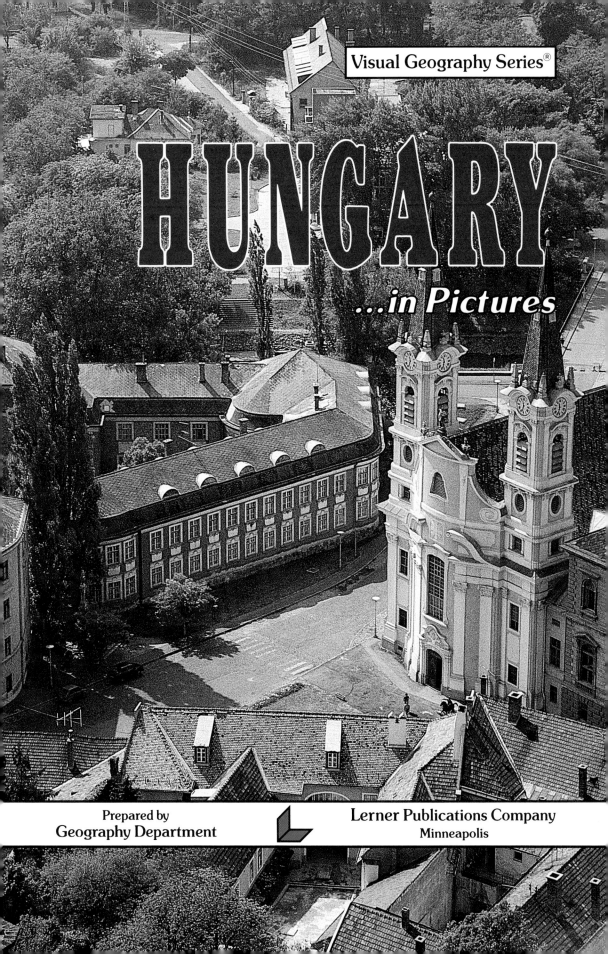

HUNGARY

...in Pictures

Prepared by
Geography Department

Lerner Publications Company
Minneapolis

Independent Picture Service

Hungarian folk dancers perform a dance in traditional shepherd's costumes.

This book is an all-new edition in the Visual Geography Series. Previous editions were published by Sterling Publishing Company, New York City. The text, set in 10/12 Century Textbook, is fully revised and updated, and new photogaphs, maps, charts, and captions have been added.

LIBRARY OF CONGRESS CATALOGING-IN-PUBLICATION DATA

Hungary in pictures / prepared by Geography Department, Lerner Publications Company.
    p. cm. — (Visual geography series)
    Includes index.
    Summary: Describes the topography, history, society, economy, and governmental structure of Hungary.
    ISBN 0-8225-1883-X (lib. bdg.)
    1. Hungary. [1. Hungary.] I. Lerner Publications Company. Geography Dept. II. Series. III. Series: Visual geography series (Minneapolis, Minn.)
DB906.H87 1993   93–3179
943.9—dc20   CIP
                                                               AC

International Standard Book Number: 0-8225-1883-X
Library of Congress Catalog Card Number: 93-3179

VISUAL GEOGRAPHY SERIES®

Publisher
Harry Jonas Lerner
Senior Editor
Mary M. Rodgers
Editors
Gretchen Bratvold
Tom Streissguth
Colleen Sexton
Photo Researcher
Erica Ackerberg
Editorial/Photo Assistant
Marybeth Campbell
Consultants/Contributors
Paul Madarasz
Paul Rupprecht
Sandra K. Davis
Designer
Jim Simondet
Cartographer
Carol F. Barrett
Indexer
Sylvia Timian
Production Manager
Gary J. Hansen

Independent Picture Service

A statue of a king stands within the Fishermen's Bastion, a part of Castle Hill in Hungary's capital city of Budapest.

Acknowledgments

Title page photo © William Weems.

Elevation contours adapted from *The Times Atlas of the World,* seventh comprehensive edition (New York: Times Books, 1985).

1 2 3 4 5 6 – I/JR – 98 97 96 95 94 93

Photo by Bernice K. Condit

Three young villagers enjoy a summer day. Adults as well as children use bicycles for short trips in the Hungarian countryside.

Contents

Introduction **7**

1) The Land **10**
Topography. Waterways. Climate. Flora and Fauna. Natural Resources. Cities.

2) History and Government **21**
Roman Settlement. The Magyars. Early Kings. Invasion and Civil War. Ottoman Attacks. Matthias Corvinus. The Protestant Reformation. Szechenyi and Kossuth. The Dual Monarchy. World War I. War and Occupation. Communism and Revolt. Democracy Arrives. Recent Events. Government.

3) The People **43**
Ethnic Heritage. Religion. Education and Health. Language and Literature. Art and Music. Food. Recreation and Sports.

4) The Economy **53**
Manufacturing. Agriculture and Forestry. Mining and Energy. Transportation and Tourism. Foreign Trade. The Future.

Index **64**

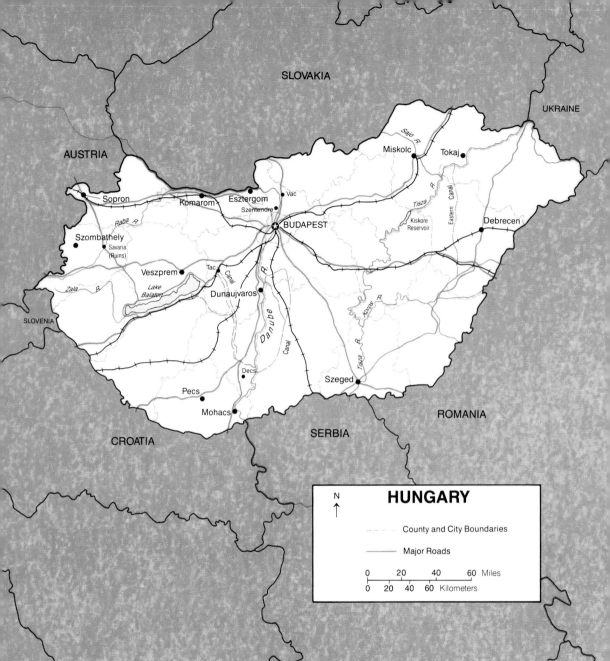

SLOVAKIA

UKRAINE

AUSTRIA

Sopron
Komarom
Esztergom
Vac
Szentendre
Miskolc
Tokaj
Sajó R.
Tisza R.
Eastern Canal
Debrecen
BUDAPEST
Kiskore Reservoir

Szombathely
Savaria (Ruins)
Raba R.

Veszprem
Tac
Canal
Lake Balaton
Danube R.
Dunaujvaros
Koros R.
Zala R.

SLOVENIA

Decs
Tisza R.
Szeged

Pecs
Mohacs

ROMANIA

CROATIA

SERBIA

HUNGARY

N

County and City Boundaries

Major Roads

0	20	40	60	Miles
0	20	40	60	Kilometers

20° 0° 20°
Arctic Circle
NORWEGIAN SEA

EUROPE
HUNGARY

0	400 Miles
0	400 Kilometers

60°
60°

NORTH ATLANTIC OCEAN

20°

40°

MEDITERRANEAN SEA

0°

20°

METRIC CONVERSION CHART
To Find Approximate Equivalents

WHEN YOU KNOW:	MULTIPLY BY:	TO FIND:
AREA		
acres	0.41	hectares
square miles	2.59	square kilometers
CAPACITY		
gallons	3.79	liters
LENGTH		
feet	30.48	centimeters
yards	0.91	meters
miles	1.61	kilometers
MASS (weight)		
pounds	0.45	kilograms
tons	0.91	metric tons
VOLUME		
cubic yards	0.77	cubic meters
TEMPERATURE		
degrees Fahrenheit	0.56 (after subtracting 32)	degrees Celsius

Traditional homes line a street in the center of Sopron, a city in north-western Hungary. Founded during the Roman occupation of Hungary, Sopron and other towns in the region contain many ethnic Germans.

Courtesy of Ibusz

Introduction

A small and landlocked nation, Hungary shares its history with both western and eastern Europe. Established in the ninth century A.D. by the Magyars—a nomadic people from the plains of Russia to the east—Hungary later linked itself to western Europe by converting to the Christian religion. Through strategic alliances and a powerful military, the Hungarian kings conquered a large territory during the 1400s and profited from agriculture, mining, and trade.

Hungary's location, however, drew the kingdom into violent conflicts in the Balkan region of southeastern Europe. In 1526 the kingdom was defeated by the Ottoman Turks, who were attacking south-eastern Europe from their base in Asia Minor (modern Turkey). By the 1540s, Hungary was divided by the Turks and by the Habsburg emperors, who ruled a huge realm from their capital at Vienna (in modern Austria). For centuries, the German-speaking Habsburgs tried to force

7

A worker examines drying sausages in a Hungarian smokehouse. Paprika, a popular reddish spice, flavors many of the country's processed meats.

their language and customs on Hungarians living under their control.

Although the Turks withdrew from Hungary by 1700, the nation remained closely linked with Austria until World War I (1914–1918), a conflict that ended the Habsburg monarchy. Hungary suffered an economic depression in the 1930s and a destructive occupation by the German army during World War II (1939–1945). After the war, the Soviet Union imposed Communist rule on Hungary and on other nations of central and eastern Europe. In 1956 a revolt against the Communist government in Budapest—Hungary's capital—resulted in an invasion by Soviet forces and in the deaths of thousands of Hungarian civilians. Not until 1989 did Hungarians throw off Communism and put in place a democratic government.

On a Hungarian farm, a well and a wooden gate stand at the entrance to a spacious yard.

Hungarian musicians perform with traditional instruments. Many of the nation's folk groups use violins and wind instruments to play sad melodies.

Hungary is now making rapid changes in its economy and its government. State-controlled firms are being sold to private owners, and Hungarian companies are trying to expand their trade with western European countries. But low productivity and inefficient factories prevent many Hungarian businesses from being competitive in the world market.

Despite centuries of foreign control and political turmoil, Hungarians have maintained a unique culture. In their language, music, and art, Hungarians—as descendants of the proud Magyars—remain distinct among the dozens of nationalities that inhabit central Europe. Although their country is experiencing a difficult transition, Hungarians are holding to their traditions in the face of an uncertain future.

The Hungarian athlete Angela Nemeth hurled a javelin during the 1968 Summer Olympics in Mexico City.

A rural village lies among rolling hills along the Sajo, a narrow stream in northeastern Hungary.

Photo by Daniel H. Condit

1) The Land

The Republic of Hungary covers 35,920 square miles, an area slightly larger than the state of Maine. The country's terrain is mostly flat, with hills and mountain ranges in the west and north. The wide Danube River flows from north to south through the center of Hungary, dividing the nation into western and eastern regions. The greatest distance from east to west is 312 miles, and from north to south Hungary stretches 193 miles.

Hungary's neighbors include Austria, in the west, and Slovakia, a nation to the north that once made up the eastern half of Czechoslovakia. Ukraine, a former republic of the old Soviet Union, borders Hungary in the northeast. Romania lies to the east and southeast. The independent nations of Serbia, Croatia, and Slovenia—which were part of the former Republic of Yugoslavia—share a frontier with southern Hungary.

Topography

Although much of central Europe is mountainous, Hungary's largest natural feature is the Nagyalfold, or Great Plain. This flat, fertile area stretches eastward from the Danube River. River valleys and small, sandy hills break up the Nagyalfold, which has been intensively farmed for centuries.

The Nagyalfold includes several smaller regions. Cumania is a sandy plain lying along the eastern bank of the Danube. Engineers have drained several of Cumania's marshlands to benefit farmers and herders. The Hortobagy, in eastern Hungary, consists of dry, flat plains known to the Hungarians as *puszta*.

North of the Nagyalfold are the Matra and Bukk mountains. These highlands make up a spur of the Carpathian Mountains, which curve through several countries in southeastern Europe. Unusual rock formations are common on the steep, thickly forested slopes of the Bukk range. Mount Kekes, the highest point in Hungary, reaches an elevation of 3,330 feet in the Matra Mountains.

Transdanubia is an area of hills, lakes, and river valleys lying west of the Danube. The Transdanubian Central Highlands cross the region and end in northern Hungary at a sharp bend of the river. The Pilis and the Borzsony hills form a narrow gorge as the river turns southward before passing Budapest.

The Bakony Mountains and the Bakony Forest lie in central Transdanubia. Inactive volcanoes and volcanic craters dot the landscape, which rises to an elevation of 2,310 feet at Mount Korishegy. The shores of Lake Balaton, a long and shallow freshwater lake, extend along the southern slopes of the Bakony range. South of the lake are rolling hills that continue to the Mecsek Mountains in the south.

The Kisalfold, or Little Plain, is an agricultural region in northwestern Hungary. West and south of the Kisalfold are the foothills of the Alps, a high mountain range that stretches westward across Austria.

Photo by Dick Nichols

Esztergom, the ancient home of Hungary's kings, rises above a bend in the wide Danube River.

Waterways

The Danube, Europe's second longest river, flows eastward along the border between Slovakia and Hungary before turning sharply to the south. The river's course takes it past Budapest and across the plains of central and southern Hungary.

An important trade route for centuries, the Danube links the nations of eastern and central Europe, where hills and mountain ranges have long hindered road and rail transportation. Barges and ferries still ply the river, carrying industrial products, minerals, and grain to ports in the Danube valley.

The Tisza River is a Danube tributary that flows through the Nagyalfold. The longest river in Hungary, the Tisza runs 360 miles before crossing into Serbia. Along the river's course in northeastern Hungary is the Kiskore Reservoir, an artificial lake that provides irrigation water to farms in the Nagyalfold.

Independent Picture Service

Tourists rest their horses near Vac, a town north of Budapest on the Danube River. A traditional religious center, Vac contains a cathedral as well as a bishop's palace.

Independent Picture Service

This bridge—one of the first to cross the Tisza River—has become a famous landmark of the Hortobagy region of eastern Hungary.

Seagoing ships wait for the ice to clear from Budapest's port on the Danube River. Although rare, floating ice can block shipping for weeks during severe winters.

The Hungarian government has built several canals to improve the country's river transportation network. The Eastern Canal, which extends into the Nagyalfold from the Tisza, irrigates the dry plains of eastern Hungary. The canal also protects farmland by draining the river during severe floods that occur in the spring.

Other Hungarian rivers include the Koros, which flows westward through southeastern Hungary, and the Raba, the major river of the Kisalfold. The Zala River and several smaller streams flow into Lake Balaton.

Climate

Most of Hungary experiences a mild climate, with warm summers and cool winters. Winds from the south and west bring warm air in the spring and summer. The Carpathian Mountains shelter the country from cold winds during the winter. Budapest averages 71°F during July, the warmest month. In January, the coldest month of winter, temperatures in the capital average 42°F.

Winters are coldest in the Nagyalfold and in the mountain ranges of northeastern Hungary. The plains of the east and south have the highest summer temperatures and in some years suffer long periods of drought.

Late spring and early summer bring heavy rains to most of Hungary. The country receives an average of about 24 inches of precipitation each year. Rains are generally heavier in the western half of the country. In the spring, melting snow from the northern highlands runs into the

Danube and its tributaries, sometimes flooding marshes in central Hungary.

Flora and Fauna

Although most of Hungary's forests have been cleared for farming, extensive woodlands have survived in mountainous regions. Government reforestation programs have created new stands of oak, ash, and beech. Deciduous (leaf-shedding) trees thrive in Transdanubia. Poplar, oak, and rowan trees grow along the Danube in southern Hungary. Willows line many of Hungary's rivers, and poplars are common on the plains near the Tisza River. The extensive root systems of acacia trees help to anchor the sandy soil of Cumania.

Farming and urban development have limited the natural habitats of Hungary's animal population. Game reserves in the northern mountains shelter small numbers

Courtesy of Hungarian Tourist Board

This flowering chestnut tree grows along the banks of the Danube River near the town of Szentendre.

Photo © William Weems

Spoonbills gather in a flooded marsh. Extensive wetlands still dot the valley of the Danube, although the construction of canals has drained many marshes and has reduced wildlife habitat.

SLOVAKIA

AUSTRIA

UKRAINE

BORZSONY
HILLS

Sajo R.

Tisza R.

KISALFOLD

PILIS
HILLS

Mt. Kekes

BUKK
MTNS.

TRANSDANUBIAN

MATRA
MTNS.

Kiskore
Reservoir

Eastern Canal

Danube R.

CENTRAL

Raba R.

Mt. Korishegy

N A G Y   A L F O L D

BAKONY   MTNS.

HIGHLANDS

HORTOBAGY

Zala R.

Canal

SLOVENIA

Lake Balaton

T R A N S D A N U B I A

Canal

Koros R.

CUMANIA

Canal

Tisza R.

ROMANIA

MECSEK
MTNS.

SERBIA

CROATIA

HUNGARY

N

Feet		Meters
		Uplands
3281 —		1000
1640 —		500 — Lowlands

0   20   40   60   Miles
0   20   40   60   Kilometers

of deer and wild boar. Eagles and falcons also survive in these highlands. Throughout Hungary, rabbits and foxes live in wooded and remote areas. Several species of migrating birds—including herons, cranes, spoonbills, and storks—nest in the marshes of the Danube valley. Freshwater fish thrive in Lake Balaton and in mountain streams.

Natural Resources

Hungary's fertile soil—one of the country's most valuable natural resources—has enabled Hungarian farmers to grow enough food for export. Mineral resources include bauxite, the raw material of aluminum, as well as manganese, which is used in steel production. Workers mine iron and copper ores in the northern mountains.

Many Hungarian cities are carefully restoring and preserving their older buildings, such as these homes on Castle Hill in Budapest.

Although deposits of crude oil and natural gas exist in the Nagyalfold and in Transdanubia, the amounts are too small to meet Hungary's energy needs. The Matra Mountains contain lignite coal, but these stocks are being rapidly exhausted, and the country is turning to other sources of energy. Uranium—the fuel used in nuclear plants—is mined in the Mecsek Mountains. The strong currents of the Danube and Tisza rivers power several hydroelectric stations.

For centuries, western Hungary was a part of the Habsburg Empire, a central European realm. Many buildings—such as this one in Sopron—were built in an architectural style popular in the Habsburg era.

Cities

Traditionally an agricultural nation, Hungary experienced a dramatic change during the twentieth century, as new industries brought farm laborers into the cities. Sixty-three percent of Hungarians now live in urban areas, which are concentrated in the nation's central and northern regions. The plains of eastern Hungary and the hills and forests of the west have lower population densities and remain mostly rural.

BUDAPEST

A city of 2.1 million people, Budapest lies along the Danube River in north cen-

tral Hungary. In 1872 the government of Hungary combined the cities of Buda and Pest—on the west and east banks of the river, respectively—to create modern Budapest.

Buda grew on the site of the ancient town of Aquincum. The city was fortified by the Hungarian leader Matthias Corvinus in the fifteenth century. After the Turks retreated from Hungary, Buda grew rapidly as both a political and cultural center. In 1867 the larger city of Pest became Hungary's capital. Five years later, Buda and Pest were united.

Budapest suffered heavy bombing as well as street fighting during World War

Courtesy of Ibusz

The Danube River divides the capital of Hungary, which includes the old cities of Buda *(left)* on the river's west bank and Pest *(right)* on the east bank. Buda and Pest were combined to form Budapest in 1872.

II. After the war, the army of the Soviet Union occupied the city. Soviet tanks again rolled through Budapest in 1956, when the city's people revolted against Hungary's Communist regime.

Budapest has become the center of banking and trade in Hungary. The capital's factories make half of Hungary's manufactured goods, which include machinery, textiles, chemicals, and electrical equipment. The hub of Hungary's road and rail networks, Budapest also has a river harbor and the country's only international airport.

The many museums, palaces, and churches of Budapest reflect the city's long history and rich architectural traditions. The magnificent Royal Palace, fully restored after suffering heavy damage

The Castle of Vajdahunyad in Budapest's City Park includes examples of Hungarian architecture from the Roman age to the eighteenth century. The castle was built in 1896 during the anniversary of 1,000 years of Hungarian nationhood.

The Great Church towers over the main square of Debrecen. In the sixteenth century, this city in northeastern Hungary became an important center of Protestant Christianity.

during World War II, rises on the steep Castle Hill in a historic quarter of Buda. Eotvos Lorant University, one of the oldest in central Europe, was founded in the city in 1635. Students in Budapest also attend several professional and technical schools.

SECONDARY CITIES

Humans have inhabited the site of Debrecen (population 220,000), the largest city of eastern Hungary, since the Stone Age. During the sixteenth century, Debrecen became a center of the religious revolt known as the Protestant Reforma-

tion. The Great Church, a large Protestant cathedral, now faces the city's main square. From the Great Church, the revolutionary leader Lajos Kossuth proclaimed Hungary's independence from the Habsburg Empire in 1849.

Located in the country's most productive agricultural region, Debrecen is a hub of food processing and livestock raising. Students from many parts of Hungary attend a prestigious agricultural institute in the city. Debrecen's factories make furniture and chemicals.

The industrial city of Miskolc (population 208,000), in northeastern Hungary,

Veszprem, a town in the Transdanubian region north of Lake Balaton, is the site of a university and a historic cathedral.

produces steel, textiles, and leather goods. Nearby vineyards supply the city's large wine-processing industry.

Szeged (population 189,000) is an important river port in southern Hungary. A massive flood of the Tisza River nearly destroyed Szeged in 1879. To celebrate the rebuilding of their city, the inhabitants raised an impressive new cathedral. Szeged now hosts an open-air music festival each summer in the cathedral square. The city's factories process timber and produce salt and paprika, a reddish spice that is an important ingredient in Hungarian cooking.

Statues, gardens, and fountains grace the central square of the city of Miskolc. Facing the square is the imposing facade of Kossuth University.

The excavation of a Roman settlement at Tac, southwest of Budapest, has uncovered two-thousand-year-old streets, foundations, and stone walls. Centered on the Italian Peninsula, Rome expanded its frontiers to the north as far as the Danube River.

2) History and Government

The hills and valleys of Transdanubia provided fertile soil and plentiful game for Hungary's prehistoric inhabitants. Archaeologists have found human remains from more than 17,000 years ago near the southern shore of Lake Balaton. Early hunters and farmers also lived along the Danube River. The Illyrians, descendants of Celtic peoples who roamed across prehistoric Europe, began settling in Hungary after 1000 B.C.

Roman Settlement

In 35 B.C., the armies of Rome, a growing empire based on the Italian Peninsula, moved north into the Danube valley. The Romans were seeking control of the

Roman settlers brought their social and religious institutions to the forests and plains of Hungary in the first century B.C. This temple in Roman Savaria (modern Szombathely) was dedicated to Isis, one of many Roman deities.

Photo by MTI Interfoto

Danube River and of the region's valuable mines. After defeating the Illyrians, the Romans established the province of Pannonia in western Hungary in 14 B.C.

To secure the empire's northern frontier, the Roman ruler Tiberius ordered the construction of fortresses and cities in Pannonia. Aquincum, the capital of Pannonia, was built on the site of modern Budapest. Other Roman settlements rose in southern and western Hungary.

Although Rome stationed strong army garrisons in the province, Pannonia suffered frequent invasions by peoples from northern and eastern Europe. Several groups attacked across the Danube in the late second century A.D. In about A.D. 430, a huge force of Asian nomads known as the Huns drove into central Europe, destroying the area's Roman settlements. After the death of their leader, Attila, the Huns retreated from Pannonia.

The repeated invasions caused the breakup of the Roman Empire in the late fifth century. Without Roman defenses, Pannonia and the rest of central Europe fell into turmoil. Sarmatians, Scythians, Bulgars, and other groups crossed into the Hungarian plains. The Avars, an Asian people, settled in the Nagyalfold and in the Danube valley.

By the sixth century, the Avars were able to bring all of Hungary under their control. But 200 years later, Charlemagne—the emperor of the Franks in western Europe—defeated the Avars and seized western Hungary. The Frankish rulers after Charlemagne set up small duchies (states ruled by dukes) in the old Roman province of Pannonia. The Nagyalfold and the highlands of the east remained sparsely populated regions inhabited by rival groups of migrating nomads.

The royal jewels of Hungary include the crown, staff, and orb of King Stephen, the tenth-century monarch who united the Magyar settlers of Hungary and converted the nation to Christianity.

Independent Picture Service

The Magyars

Arriving in the 890s from lands east of the Carpathian Mountains, the Magyars attacked and destroyed the scattered settlements on the Hungarian plains. The Magyars were grouped into seven independent bands, each of which was made up of several clans (groups of families). Under Arpad—the strongest of the seven chiefs—these bands established a Magyar nation in 896.

For several decades, the Magyars pressed their attacks on France, Italy and Germany. They raided cities and villages, looting property and taking captives for ransom or as slaves. But in 955, the

Photo by Bernice K. Condit

Castle Diosgyor was built in the tenth century near Miskolc. An important stronghold of the Hungarian kings, the castle was destroyed in the 1400s when the Ottoman Turks invaded Hungary.

German king Otto I rallied a large force and stopped the Magyars at the Lech River, in what is now Germany. After this defeat, the Magyars returned to Hungary and began to form alliances with other nations, including the kingdom of Bavaria in southern Germany.

By the tenth century, the Roman Catholic Church had converted many of the peoples of central Europe to Christianity. (This faith had become the official religion of the Roman Empire and had survived the empire's fall.) In 975 the Magyar leader Geza—a descendant of Arpad—and other members of the Arpad family were baptized as Christians. Missionaries of the pope, the head of the Roman Catholic Church, were spreading the religion throughout Hungary. Nevertheless, many Magyars refused to accept Christianity. The nation was still divided, and the Arpad dynasty (family of rulers) competed with other Magyar chiefs for control.

Early Kings

After Geza's death, his son Stephen sought recognition for the Magyar nation from the Catholic pope, one of Europe's most powerful leaders. During a ceremony in Esztergom—the site of the Arpad palace—on Christmas Day, 1000, Stephen was crowned king of Hungary. The pope recognized the ceremony and allowed Stephen to establish a Hungarian church. In return, Stephen made Christianity the official religion of his realm.

King Stephen's ambition was to make Hungary the equal of the most powerful states of Europe. After gathering an army of knights and foot soldiers, he defeated his rivals among the Magyar chiefs and united the Magyar bands under his authority. The Hungarians converted to Christianity, and Stephen established a strong royal administration. The king divided Hungary into counties and appointed officials to collect taxes and to serve as judges.

The independent Magyar chiefs acknowledge King Stephen's authority over the land of Hungary. Stephen united his realm by force and gained the recognition of the pope, the powerful leader of the Roman Catholic Church.

Artwork by Laura Westlund

Through marriage alliances and military conquests, the kings of Hungary's Arpad dynasty (family of rulers) built the country into one of the largest realms in Europe. By the early 1200s, Hungary stretched from the Adriatic Sea in the south to Bohemia in the north and to Transylvania in the east.

Although the king was successful in organizing the Magyar nation, the descendants of the Magyar chiefs still controlled extensive private lands. These nobles swore loyalty to the king, to whom they owed military service during wartime. But the nobles also formed an independent council that advised the king on important matters. The landowners and the Hungarian monarchs remained rivals for political power for centuries.

Laszlo I, who assumed the throne in 1077, sought to increase Hungary's territory, which Stephen had extended eastward into Transylvania. Through a marriage alliance, Laszlo brought Croatia, a region to the south, under his control. Laszlo's successors expanded Hungary's borders southward to the Adriatic Sea and eastward to territories in the Balkan Peninsula. With its good harvests, valuable minerals, and secure borders, Hungary began to attract immigrants from many parts of Europe.

Courtesy of Hungarian Commercial Counsellor

The Millenary Monument in Budapest carries the figure of Arpad, the founder of the Arpad dynasty, atop its central stone column. On either side, a colonnade frames bronze statues of Hungary's kings and national leaders.

Although Hungary was growing rapidly, the kingdom was often thrown into chaos by disputes over the royal succession. Many Hungarian leaders also weakened the state through their greed and ambition. In the 1200s the corrupt king Endre (Andras) II began selling royal land and privileges to his supporters.

Alarmed at the actions of the king, Hungary's nobles forced him to sign a charter known as the Golden Bull in 1222. This document ended taxes on the landowners and allowed the nobles to disobey any king who acted illegally. In addition, wealthy landowners were no longer required to join the king on his foreign campaigns.

Invasion and Civil War

The Arpad dynasty had built a large and strong kingdom, but Hungary was still vulnerable to outside attack. In the 1240s, a huge army of Mongol warriors crossed the Carpathian Mountains from the east. Although Bela IV, the Hungarian king, pleaded for help from other European rulers, no reinforcements arrived. The Mongols destroyed the Hungarian forces but retreated in 1242 after the death of one of their leaders. Bela then ordered fortifications to be built around several Hungarian cities to protect the kingdom from future attacks.

Despite Bela's efforts to strengthen Hungary, the Arpad dynasty gradually declined after his death in 1270. When the last Arpad king died without a male heir in 1301, Hungary was thrown into a violent civil war over the succession. Several powerful nobles, each of whom possessed a private army, fought for the right to select Hungary's future king.

In 1308 the nobles finally agreed to elect Charles Robert, a member of the Angevin dynasty of Anjou in France, to be king of Hungary. Ruling as Charles I, he restored order in the realm, which had suffered widespread destruction during the civil war.

Independent Picture Service

The Mongol chief Batu Khan invaded eastern Europe and captured the Hungarian city of Pest in 1241. The Mongol forces quickly retreated, however, after the death of one of their leaders in Asia.

By selecting loyal ministers to direct local affairs, Charles created a new class of powerful government officials. He also introduced the feudal landowning system that was common in France. Under this system, feudal serfs (landless peasants) became the property of landowners, to whom the serfs owed their labor and a portion of their crops each year. The serfs could not leave the land they farmed.

Under Charles's successors, Hungary grew wealthy from trade and from gold mining in Transylvania. Lajos I, the son of Charles I, was a skillful commander who conquered several neighboring states. The Angevin kings also used legal and financial reforms to gain the loyalty of merchants and lesser nobles. Nevertheless, Hungary's most powerful nobles, known as "magnates," remained independent.

Ottoman Attacks

Many of the gains made by Lajos were in jeopardy by the end of the fourteenth century, as Hungary faced an attack by the Ottoman Turks. In the 1350s, the Turks had crossed into the Balkan Peninsula from their base in Asia Minor. To meet this threat, Lajos ordered the construction of new fortifications around Hungary's cities and mining towns. Lajos defeated the Turks on the battlefield in 1377.

But the Ottoman armies were bringing much of southeastern Europe under their control. In most Balkan regions, the Ottoman sultan (emperor) allowed local rulers to remain in power as long as they paid tribute (money) to the Ottoman treasury. Many of these European princes were also willing to ally with the Ottoman sultan against Hungary.

The Hungarian prince Sigismund Janos kneels before Suleiman the Magnificent, the sultan (ruler) of the Ottoman Empire. The Turks governed conquered lands in eastern and central Europe through obedient local officials who provided money and soldiers to the sultan.

Courtesy of Cultural and Tourism Office of the Turkish Embassy

Independent Picture Service

Janos Hunyadi leads the defense of Belgrade (in modern Serbia) against the forces of the Ottoman Empire in 1456. Although Hunyadi died shortly after the battle, his victory temporarily saved Hungary and much of central Europe from the Turks.

Photo by MTI Interfoto

King Matthias Corvinus, the son of Janos Hunyadi, recruited a strong army to defend Hungary from Ottoman attacks. A patron of science and literature, Matthias established the Bibliotheca Corvina, one of the largest libraries in Europe.

Lajos's successor, Sigismund, enlisted Hungary's feudal barons to join a crusade against the Ottoman Empire. Before his death in 1437, he also required all Hungarian towns to provide a cavalry force for defense against the Turks.

Heading the Hungarian army was Janos Hunyadi, a skilled military leader who was the son of one of Sigismund's knights. Hunyadi defeated the Turks in Transylvania and gained the support of the Hungarian nobles. In 1446 a parliament of lesser nobles assembled and, in defiance of Hungary's magnates, elected Hunyadi as the governor of Hungary.

Hunyadi fortified Belgrade (in modern Serbia) and stopped the Turks at the gates of the city in 1456. But the Hungarian leader died a few weeks after his victory. The nobles met again two years later and proclaimed Hunyadi's son Matthias as the new king.

28

Matthias Corvinus

Matthias, who was nicknamed Corvinus (the Raven), recruited immigrants and mercenaries (hired soldiers) to establish a permanent military force. He used this army to defend Hungary against the Turks, to collect taxes from the magnates, and to stop rebellions by Hungarian peasants. By drawing up a new code of laws, Matthias earned a reputation among his subjects as a just ruler. A patron of the arts and education, he built a lavish palace in Buda and founded several universities.

Matthias helped the growth of towns by improving transportation and by opening trade with foreign nations. Hungary exported wine and food, and the region's abundant mineral resources—including iron, tin, and copper—brought in great wealth. The growth of Hungary's cities, which enthusiastically supported the king, balanced the power of the realm's wealthy magnates, who opposed paying taxes to the king's treasury.

After the death of Matthias Corvinus in 1490, the nobles and magnates agreed to elect Laszlo II—the ruler of the small realm of Bohemia to the north—as the Hungarian king. A weak monarch, Laszlo gave in to the demands of the nobles to repeal taxes. As a result, the kingdom grew poorer and more unstable. The strong army raised by Matthias Corvinus fell into decline, leaving Hungary vulnerable to the Turks.

Faced with another Turkish offensive in the 1520s, Lajos II—Laszlo's successor—failed to reinforce the Hungarian army or to strengthen his realm's defenses. In 1526, after setting out with a small army, Lajos was defeated by the Turks at the southern Hungarian town of Mohacs. Lajos and most of his troops were killed in the battle.

With no army to stop them, the Turks invaded the Nagyalfold and the Danube valley, burning estates and driving away peasants and landowners. The Turkish conquest split Hungary into three parts. Transylvania became an independent principality (domain of a prince). The sultan added central Hungary to the Ottoman Empire. The Habsburg Empire—a realm that covered territory to the west and south—seized western Hungary to defend against Turkish attacks.

Independent Picture Service

A magnificent palace *(left)* built by Matthias Corvinus dominated the skyline of Buda in the late fifteenth century. During the Turkish occupation of Buda, however, the palace fell into ruins.

The Protestant Reformation

After the Turkish conquest of central Hungary, military and religious conflict continued in Europe. In Germany, Martin Luther was leading a movement for reform of the Catholic church. Many of the German immigrants living in Hungary joined Luther's new Protestant church. Gabor Bethlen, the prince of Transylvania in the early 1600s, allowed Protestants in his principality to worship freely.

The Habsburg emperors, however, remained loyal to the Catholic church. Although many Hungarian nobles and townspeople were converting to Protestantism, the Habsburg armies frequently attacked Protestant churches and clergy. Bethlen retaliated by fighting the Habsburg forces and by supporting the Protestants in central Europe. Eventually, the clash of Catholics and Protestants led to the Thirty Years' War, an international conflict that lasted from 1618 until 1648.

Bethlen's military successes prompted the Hungarian parliament to elect him Hungary's leader in 1620. In the next year, Bethlen signed a treaty with the Habsburg rulers. He renounced his title but added a large territory to the domain of Transylvania. Although Transylvania remained Protestant, missionaries converted most of the powerful Hungarian nobles back to Catholicism.

In the late seventeenth century, the Habsburgs allied with Poland to fight the Ottoman Empire. In 1683 the Turks were defeated during a siege of Vienna, the Habsburg capital in Austria. Three years later, Turkish forces retreated from Buda. By 1700 the Habsburg army had driven the Turks from Hungary and had taken control of Transylvania.

Courtesy of Minneapolis Public Library and Information Center

The Hofburg palace in Vienna, Austria, was the seat of power for the rulers of the Habsburg Empire. After the Turkish retreat from central Europe, Austrian forces occupied much of Hungary and the Habsburgs made themselves Hungary's hereditary rulers.

The Transylvanian prince Gabor Bethlen, a Protestant, clashed frequently with the Catholic Habsburg rulers. Although he was elected king of Hungary in 1620, he soon gave up the title and made peace with the Habsburgs.

Photo by MTI Interfoto

Despite their defeat of the Turks, the Habsburgs were not interested in the freedom of Hungary. Instead, they attempted to turn the country into a loyal, German-speaking nation. The Hungarians were forced to accept the Habsburgs as their hereditary rulers. The Habsburgs also allowed foreign immigrants to seize Hungarian estates in areas reconquered from the Turks.

In 1703 the unpopular policies of the Habsburg administration drove the Hungarians to revolt. Led by Ferenc Rakoczi II, the rebellion lasted eight years, and Rakoczi's forces nearly reached Vienna. In 1711, after a defeat of the rebels, the Habsburg emperor offered a peace treaty. The Hungarian assembly, or diet, was allowed to meet. The emperor also promised religious freedom in Hungary.

HABSBURG REFORMS

As Hungary gradually recovered from the years of war and occupation, the Habsburgs changed their policies and agreed to respect Hungary's laws and constitution. In the 1740s—when the Habsburg empress Maria Theresa went to war against Prussia (a German kingdom in northern Europe)—she asked for help from the Hungarian assembly. An elite force of Hungarian cavalry soldiers known as *huszars* answered this appeal and joined the Habsburg army.

In gratitude for this aid, Maria Theresa declared Transylvania to be a grand duchy of the Habsburg Empire. This action allowed some independence to the Hungarians of Transylvania. Although she kept firm control over the rest of Hungary, the empress built a new system

Habsburg soldiers ride through the Hungarian countryside during the reign of Empress Maria Theresa.

of schools and in 1767 passed a decree allowing Hungarian peasants to move freely about the country.

Maria Theresa's son, Joseph II, attempted to reorganize Hungary for the purpose of ruling it directly from Vienna. He abolished local assemblies in the Hungarian counties and declared German to be the nation's official language. After Joseph's death in 1790, his successor restored Hungary's constitution. As a part of the Habsburg Empire, however, Hungary was still expected to support the realm with taxes and with soldiers in wartime. In the early 1800s, when Habsburg armies fought against the French leader Napoleon, heavy taxation caused growing dissent within Hungary.

Szechenyi and Kossuth

The opposition movement gathered strength in Hungary under Count Istvan Szechenyi, a former officer of the huszars.

Szechenyi called for sweeping social and economic reforms. In 1825, to help promote his goals, he founded the Academy of Sciences. Speaking against the old feudal system, Szechenyi argued for higher taxes on the nobles and for the complete freedom of Hungary's serfs. At the same time, he wanted Hungary to remain within the Habsburg Empire.

The Habsburg monarchy responded to the rising discontent by arresting several reformers, including the lawyer Lajos Kossuth. A brilliant and fiery speaker, Kossuth demanded freedom for the serfs, the right of commoners to vote, an overhaul of the tax system, and independence. After gaining his release from prison, Kossuth called for armed resistance to the Habsburg government. With their opposing views on the proper road to reform, Szechenyi and Kossuth became bitter enemies.

In the spring of 1848, popular rebellions swept through many European capitals.

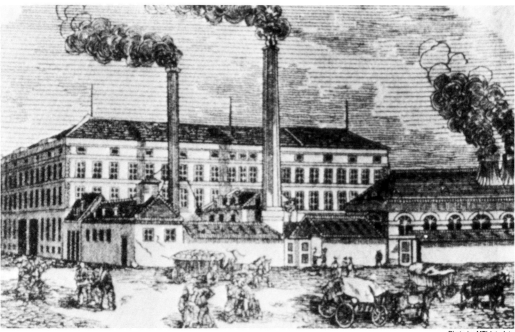

Photo by MTI Interfoto

In the early nineteenth century, busy factories and mills in Buda employed a growing class of urban industrial workers. Although the country was rapidly modernizing, the strict rule of the Habsburgs led to increasing discontent in the cities.

Photo by MTI Interfoto

Hungarian and Habsburg soldiers clash during the revolution of 1848. Hungary's skilled generals could not overcome the strength of the Habsburg armies, which crushed the revolt in 1849.

On March 15, the poet Sandor Petofi led a revolt in the Hungarian city of Pest. Kossuth, Szechenyi, and several colleagues put aside their differences to form a government that adopted a program of tax, land, and social reforms. The new regime also proclaimed that Transylvania was now part of Hungary.

In the fall of 1848, anti-Habsburg riots broke out in Vienna. The emperor Ferdinand gave up his throne and was succeeded by his nephew Franz Joseph. The Hungarian government, led by Kossuth, refused to recognize Franz Joseph's authority and prepared to fight. Throughout the winter and spring of 1849, the Hungarian army won a series of victories against Habsburg forces. In April the Hungarian parliament formally proclaimed independence for Hungary.

At the same time, the czar (emperor) of Russia—a huge empire lying east of Hungary—was offering help to Franz Joseph. In the summer of 1849, the armies

Courtesy of Library of Congress

In fiery speeches and eloquent articles, Lajos Kossuth demanded liberty for the Hungarians from Habsburg rule. The failure of the revolt of 1848 led to Kossuth's permanent exile from Hungary.

One of Hungary's most famous landmarks is the Chain Bridge, which links historic Buda and Pest. Symbolic of the capital's unification in 1872, the bridge was heavily damaged during World War II and was later rebuilt.

Courtesy of Hungarian Commercial Counsellor

of Austria and Russia attacked Hungary from the west and north. Outnumbered and surrounded, the Hungarian army surrendered in August. As Kossuth and many members of his government fled the country, the Habsburgs captured and executed 13 revolutionary leaders.

The Dual Monarchy

After defeating Hungary, Franz Joseph put the nation under the control of an imperial council and placed foreign officials in charge of Hungary's counties. Although the emperor struck down most of Kossuth's reforms, the new government improved Hungary's transportation system by building roads and railroads.

Nevertheless, opposition to rule by the Habsburgs continued within Hungary. Seeking to resolve the conflict, Franz Joseph granted the nation an independent, elected parliament in 1865. Two years later, a new constitution was drawn up, making Hungary an independent state with its own laws and government. The head of government would be a Hungarian prime minister. By this act, the Habsburg Empire became the dual monarchy of Austria-Hungary.

Two strong political groups formed in Hungary. One favored the new union with Austria. The other, following Kossuth's ideas, demanded complete independence. For many years, the divided government was unable to decide on important laws, and the Hungarian economy declined.

In 1876 Kalman Tisza became Hungary's prime minister. A strong-willed politician, Tisza reformed the educational system and improved the country's economy. He also attempted to unify the nation—which included several different ethnic groups—by requiring the use of the Hungarian language in official matters.

During Tisza's reign, Hungary's economy grew rapidly as busy factories drew industrial workers from the countryside into the cities. The rail network was extended, and Hungarian companies profited from trade with other European nations. Tisza's strict leadership, however, drew criticism from his opponents, and in 1890 he resigned from the government.

Although the nation was rapidly developing, the many changes caused social problems. By the end of the nineteenth century, Hungary's ethnic minorities—including Serbs, Slovaks, Croatians, and Germans—were pressing the government for greater control over their affairs. In addition, factory laborers who had to work long days in poor conditions began striking in the cities. A new political group, the General Workers party, organized to demand better pay and shorter workdays.

World War I

Nationalist conflicts were also brewing in other parts of the Habsburg Empire. Bosnia—a Habsburg territory south of Hungary—was seeking greater freedom from Austrian control. In the summer of 1914, the heir to the Habsburg throne was assassinated in Bosnia. The shooting, and a complex system of international alliances, led to a world war, with Russia, France, Italy, and Britain fighting Austria-Hungary, Germany, and Turkey.

Within Hungary, many workers and ethnic minorities opposed World War I. Strikes and demonstrations threatened the Hungarian government, which was divided in its support of Austria. In 1918 the Independence party, under its leader Count Mihaly Karolyi, demanded an end to Hungarian involvement in the war, as well as a program of land reform and complete independence from Austria.

After suffering defeat in Italy and in the Balkan Peninsula, Austria surrendered in 1918. The Habsburg Empire broke apart, an event that led to the creation of Czechoslovakia to the north and of Yugoslavia to the south. In November, a violent revolt in Budapest overthrew the Hungarian government. A new republic was founded under the leadership of Count Karolyi.

Hungary remained unstable as new revolutionary parties—including Socialists and Communists—gained strength and forced Count Karolyi to resign. A Hungarian soviet (ruling committee) soon took power under the leadership of the Communist politician Bela Kun. The Communists,

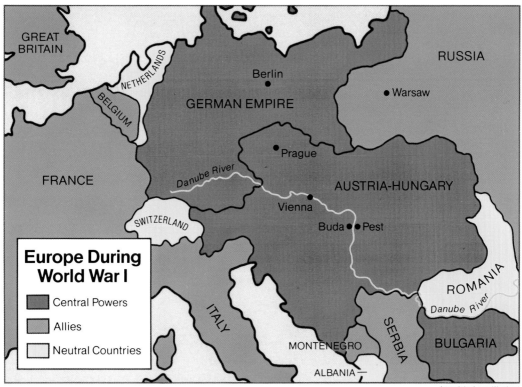

Artwork by Laura Westlund

World War I (1914–1918) pitted Austria-Hungary (the former Habsburg Empire) and Germany against Russia, France, Britain, and Italy. Many Hungarians, however, strongly opposed fighting for Austria. The defeat of Austria-Hungary and Germany led to the breakup of the historic Habsburg realm and to the founding of a new Hungarian republic. The war also helped Communist revolutionaries to topple the Russian Empire and, in 1922, to establish the Soviet Union.

Wounded soldiers gather in the streets of Budapest after the end of World War I. Many unemployed Hungarian veterans joined the strikes and demonstrations that plagued Hungary during the 1920s.

who believed in state control of all property, seized many of the country's banks and heavy industries. In Russia, a Communist party had already overthrown the Russian government and would soon establish the Soviet Union.

HORTHY'S REGIME

At the same time, Hungary was under attack by Romania, which was fighting for control of Transylvania. When Romanian forces occupied Budapest, Kun's government fell from power. After the Romanians withdrew from the capital, the Hungarian parliament declared the nation to be a kingdom. Admiral Miklos Horthy, a popular military leader, was chosen to rule Hungary as regent (one who rules in place of a monarch).

The new nations of southeastern Europe were still competing for control of large territories, including Transylvania. In June 1920, to settle these disputes, Hungarian diplomats agreed to the Treaty of Trianon. By the treaty's terms, Hungary lost huge tracts of land and much of its population to Czechoslovakia and to Yugoslavia. In addition, the treaty made Transylvania a part of Romania.

During the 1920s, Hungary's weak government did little to combat economic and social turmoil. As prices rose rapidly, the Hungarian currency lost most of its value. Unemployment and tension among Hungary's many ethnic groups caused strikes and riots. In the fall of 1931, the worsening economic depression forced Hungary's prime minister to resign. To replace him,

Admiral Horthy appointed the conservative leader Gyula Gombos.

War and Occupation

In 1933 the Nazi regime of Adolf Hitler took power in Germany. Seeking an alliance with Hungary, Hitler promised Gombos that he would return lands lost by Hungary in the Treaty of Trianon. Gombos, in exchange, sought to establish a nationalist Hungarian party allied with the Nazis. Germany invested in Hungarian industries and helped Hungary to rearm itself with modern weapons.

Hitler invaded Czechoslovakia in 1938 and forced the Czech government to give up land to Hungary. In the next year, Hitler attacked western Poland—an action that triggered World War II. At first, the Hungarian government stayed out of the conflict, but in 1941 Hungary allowed German armies to cross its territory to invade the Balkan Peninsula. In the summer of 1941, Hungarian forces joined the German attack on the Soviet Union. The Soviets had allied with Britain and France to fight Germany and Italy.

By 1944 Germany was retreating from the Soviet Union. Sensing a German defeat, Hungary's leaders tried to compromise with the Allies. These negotiations prompted the Germans to invade Hungary. At the same time, Soviet armies were sweeping through eastern and central Europe, forcing the Germans to fall back. After reaching Hungary, the Soviets set up a provisional (temporary) Communist government in Debrecen.

As World War II ended in May 1945, the Soviet army was occupying Hungary and several other nations in the region.

Bombing and street fighting heavily damaged Budapest, which was under both German and Soviet occupation during World War II. To slow the advance of the Soviet forces, the Germans destroyed all of the city's bridges in 1944.

In 1956 demonstrators gathered on the first day of the anti-Communist uprising in Budapest. Soviet tanks and troops eventually defeated the rebellion—the first violent outbreak in central Europe against Communist rule.

Photo by MTI Interfoto

The presence of Soviet forces allowed the Hungarian Communist party to take control of the government. The Communists began seizing Hungary's mines and factories from their owners. In addition, the party banned publications and organizations that opposed the new Communist leaders.

Communism and Revolt

The Hungarian Communist party—under its leader Matyas Rakosi—wrote a new constitution in 1949 that closely followed the constitution of the Soviet Union. All private industries were nationalized (placed under government control), and Hungarian peasants were forced to join state-run collective farms. The government used prison camps and an extensive network of police spies to punish opposition.

In the early 1950s, Hungary's economy began to weaken under inefficient government management. After Rakosi had several disagreements with the Soviet government, Soviet leaders forced him from his post. In 1953 Imre Nagy took over Rakosi's position.

Despite the change in leadership, many Hungarians were unhappy with the Communist regime and with the country's weak economy. In 1956 demonstrations broke out in Budapest and in many other cities. Nagy responded by freeing political prisoners and the head of Hungary's Catholic church. In defiance of the Soviet Union, he also declared Hungary a neutral country. Several units of the Hungarian army joined the rebels in the capital.

In response, the Soviet leader Nikita Khrushchev ordered an invasion of Hungary. Soviet tanks attacked demonstrators in Budapest, and street fighting killed thousands. As the revolt failed, Nagy went into hiding. After surrendering, Nagy was executed in 1958.

The Soviets appointed Janos Kadar, a loyal Communist official, as the new leader of Hungary. They allowed Kadar to make some changes in the state-controlled economy and to form closer trading ties with western Europe. In 1968 the Hungarian government introduced the New Economic Mechanism, which permitted some companies to operate without state interference.

As trade with western Europe increased, the standard of living in Hungary gradually improved. Nevertheless, the rising price of fuels and important raw materials burdened Hungary's economy. Still fearing the power of the Soviet Union, which disapproved of many of his reforms, Kadar refused to further loosen central control. His caution led to more shortages of consumer goods.

Photo by MTI Interfoto

Although Communist party leader Janos Kadar made some economic reforms, he was careful to cooperate with the powerful Soviet Union, which opposed any changes in the Communist system.

The colors of the Hungarian flag have deep historical roots. Red was the traditional color of Arpad, who led the Magyars into central Europe in the ninth century. White symbolizes King Stephen, the founder of the Hungarian kingdom. The color green has been associated with the Hungarian state since the 1400s. Hungary borrowed the three-banded design from the French revolutionary *tricolour,* which stood for antiroyalist, nationalist movements in the mid-1800s.

Artwork by Laura Westlund

Democracy Arrives

During the 1980s, many Communist regimes in Europe began to experience worsening social turmoil. Workers demanded a greater voice in running their companies. Students and writers protested governmental censorship. In May 1988, the Hungarian Communist party replaced Janos Kadar with Karoly Grosz. A few months later, Grosz stepped down and was replaced by Miklos Nemeth. For the first time in more than 40 years, non-Communist political parties began openly vying for power in Hungary.

The Soviet Union, which was attempting to deal with turmoil within its own borders, could not control the new parties in Hungary. In 1989 the Hungarian government officially declared the execution of Imre Nagy to be illegal. In a symbolic act that demonstrated Hungary's break with its Communist past, Nagy was reburied with full honors.

In October 1989, the government authored sweeping changes in Hungary's constitution. The revised document established the elected office of president and set up a National Assembly, which would be open to non-Communist representatives. Shortly afterward, the government officially proclaimed the founding of the Republic of Hungary.

Courtesy of General Electric

The Hungarian government allows foreign firms to invest in manufacturing businesses, such as this U.S.-operated light-bulb factory near Budapest. By employing Hungarian workers, these joint ventures ease the unemployment caused by economic restructuring.

The Hungarian National Assembly meets in Parliament House, a Budapest landmark that dates to the nineteenth century.

Recent Events

In open elections held in 1990, the Hungarian Democratic Forum won 37 percent of the popular vote and the largest number of seats in the National Assembly. The Communists, who had renamed themselves the Hungarian Socialist party, finished fourth. The Democratic Forum formed a coalition government that elected Jozsef Antall as the Hungarian prime minister.

The Hungarian Communist party quickly lost power, and the Soviet Union withdrew its troops from Hungary. Unlike other countries that had experienced several decades of Communist rule, Hungary had peacefully made the transition to democracy and a parliamentary system.

To improve trade, Antall and Arpad Goncz, the Hungarian president, have fostered closer relations with western European countries. Hungary is applying for membership in the European Community, which unites several European countries in a common market. Hungary's government is also trying to attract foreign investors by encouraging joint ventures and by selling state-owned businesses. But the long and difficult process of reforming the economy has just begun.

Government

The Hungarian government revised the nation's constitution in 1989. The 386 members of the Hungarian National Assembly now have the power to propose laws and amendments to the constitution. Citizens 18 years of age and older elect assembly members, who serve a term of four years. The passage of laws requires approval by a majority of the assembly's members, but constitutional changes require a two-thirds majority. The assembly also has the power to enact economic programs, to declare war, and to draw up a national budget.

The National Assembly elects Hungary's president, who is the head of state and the commander in chief of the armed forces. The president serves a term of four years and may be elected to a second term. The chief executive may conclude treaties, propose legislation, and appoint diplomats and military officers.

The president also recommends the candidates for the Council of Ministers, which consists of 18 ministers who must be approved by the National Assembly. They direct the various government ministries and supervise action on the government's economic plans. The chairperson of the council acts as Hungary's prime minister.

Hungary's judicial system changed little during the country's transition from Communist to democratic government. A supreme court is the highest court of appeal. County and district courts judge local cases.

Hungary is divided into 25 counties, 6 of which are cities. A council, whose members are elected to four-year terms, governs each county and city. Elected councils also direct Hungary's smaller towns and villages.

Photo by MTI Interfoto

A huge crowd attends the reburial of Imre Nagy, a ceremony that helped to usher in Hungary's democratic government. Nagy's execution after the revolt of 1956 had symbolized the injustices of one-party rule in Hungary.

Bathers enjoy the thermal baths at an elegant hotel in Budapest. Heated underground reservoirs supply Hungary's famous medicinal spas. The hotel also offers steam baths and outdoor, cold-water pools.

Photo by Renata Polt

3) The People

A nation of 10.3 million people, Hungary is home to several ethnic groups. More than 90 percent of the people, however, are of Magyar origin and speak the Hungarian language. Many Hungarians have moved from the countryside into the cities since World War II, and two-thirds of the nation's people now live in urban areas.

Hungary's rate of population growth, which was stable for many years, turned negative in the 1990s. With a death rate slightly higher than its birthrate, the country is experiencing a slow population decline.

Ethnic Heritage

Arriving in Europe from central Asia in the ninth century, the Magyars settled in the plains of Hungary and in neighboring regions. Hungarians still live in Slovakia, Croatia, and Serbia. In addition, more than

Women from the countryside offer clothing and embroidery for sale on the streets of Budapest. With the government no longer controlling prices and production, an open market for goods of all kinds flourishes in the capital.

two million ethnic Hungarians inhabit Transylvania, which is now a part of Romania.

Germans, who number nearly 300,000, are the largest ethnic minority within Hungary. German-speaking merchants and traders began settling in Hungarian towns during the Arpad dynasty. After the retreat of the Ottoman Turks in the late 1600s, Germans moved into the sparsely populated plains of southeastern Hungary. The descendants of these German immigrants have adapted to Hungarian society, and most now speak Hungarian as their first language.

Slovenes, Croatians, and Serbs—Slavic peoples from regions south of Hungary— live near Hungary's border with the former republic of Yugoslavia. Hungary also has a small population of Slovaks, whose his-

toric home is in the hills and forests to the north. Romanians inhabit villages near Hungary's frontier with Transylvania. The Hungarian population includes about 200,000 Gypsies, who live in small settlements and in the outskirts of urban areas.

Religion

Hungary has been a Christian nation since the tenth century, when King Stephen converted to Roman Catholicism. The Catholic church remains strong in western Hungary, which was ruled by the Catholic Habsburgs. Other branches of Christianity have gained followers in the years since the Protestant Reformation. The Reformed Church, a Protestant denomination centered in Debrecen, is the second largest church in the nation.

Many of the country's Germans are members of the Lutheran Church, which began in Germany in the sixteenth century. Other, smaller Protestant sects include Baptists, Methodists, and Adventists. Hungary's Serbs belong to the Eastern Orthodox Church.

The occupation of Hungary by German forces during World War II devastated the country's Jewish population. The Germans deported thousands of Jewish families to concentration camps in Germany and Poland. After the war, many Hungarian Jews settled in Israel, a Middle Eastern nation. Nevertheless, the Jewish neighborhood in Budapest survived the war, as did an important Jewish seminary (religious school). Jews in Hungary now number about 80,000.

After Hungary's Communist regime came to power in the late 1940s, the government placed new restrictions on religious practice. The government seized church property and forced the leaders of the various religions in Hungary to resign their offices.

During the 1980s, the government eased its policies. Private religious schools are operating, and the country's churches publish books and magazines. The new government that came to power in 1990 ended all legal controls over religion.

A church spire, and a decorated cross, rise above the streets of Szentendre. Once under the control of the Habsburgs, Szentendre is predominantly Roman Catholic.

Photo © Guy C. Galambos

45

Education and Health

The Hungarian Communist government transformed the education system after World War II, using the system of the Soviet Union as a model. The state requires all children to attend 10 years of school and provides most education free of charge. Although the government supports academic and professional schools, many students prepare for specific occupations with vocational training.

Education for Hungarian children begins in kindergartens—or *ovoda* in Hungarian—for children from three to six years of age. Although attendance at the ovoda is not required, nearly 90 percent of Hungarian parents send their children to these schools.

Elementary school starts at age six and continues until age fourteen. Primary schools teach general subjects as well as some practical skills. Students then enter a two-year continuation school or a four-year secondary school. Gymnasiums (secondary schools) offer academic subjects, and vocational schools emphasize job training in agricultural or industrial careers. With 10 years of schooling now required, about 98 percent of Hungary's population is literate. Bilingual (two-language) schools have been established in southern Hungary, where many ethnic Slavs do not use Hungarian as their everyday language.

Hungary has more than 70 postsecondary institutions, including universities, medical colleges, and technical schools. To gain admittance, students must pass four years of secondary school and a difficult entrance examination. The largest universities are in Budapest, Pecs, Szeged, and Debrecen.

Photo by MTI Interfoto

First-grade schoolchildren learn the alphabet by spelling out the Hungarian word for "shield."

Photo © Guy C. Galambos

A large house shelters a family in Komarom, a town on Hungary's border with Slovakia. Many ethnic Hungarians still inhabit the Czech Republic as well as Slovakia. Their demands for political independence and closer ties to Hungary have caused tensions among the three nations.

In the years after the war, Hungary's Communist government built new health clinics in rural areas, where many villages had lacked doctors and medical facilities. The health-care system benefited from state-supported professional training for doctors and nurses. By the early 1990s, life expectancy in Hungary had reached 69 years, an average figure for the formerly Communist nations of Europe. The infant mortality rate—the number of babies that die before reaching their first birthday—stood at 15 per 1,000 live births. This figure is also average among Hungary's neighbors.

Sidewalk tables offer tourists a place to rest on Castle Hill in Budapest.

Photo by Renata Polt

Language and Literature

The Hungarian language belongs to the Finno-Ugric group, a family of languages that originated in central Russia. Finnish and Estonian are the only other Finno-Ugric languages in Europe. Hungarian has borrowed words from Slavic languages, from German, from Latin, and from Turkish. Although various dialects of Hungarian exist, Hungarian-speakers from different regions of the country can easily understand one another. In addition, many Hungarians speak second languages, the most common being German and English.

For centuries after the conversion of Hungary to Roman Catholicism, Latin was the official language of the Hungarian government. During the fifteenth century, Hungarians began to publish books. A Latin-Hungarian dictionary appeared in 1539, and two years later Hungarian scholars translated the New Testament into their own language. Balint Balassi, a poet of the sixteenth century, was one of the first authors to write in Hungarian.

Many Hungarian writers of the 1700s and 1800s strongly opposed the rule of their country by the Habsburg emperors, who attempted to make German the official language of Hungary. The poet Ferenc Kazinczy (1759–1831) resisted this policy and worked to modernize the Hungarian language. Mihaly Vorosmarty supported Hungary's revolution through epic historical novels, plays, and poems. Sandor Petofi, who is considered the country's national poet, wrote patriotic and lyrical Hungarian verse in the mid-nineteenth century. Janos Arany, one of Hungary's best-known lyric poets, wrote an epic poem about the legendary Hungarian hero Toldi. This author also translated the plays of William Shakespeare into Hungarian.

Hungary's modern writers mastered a variety of fictional forms, including short stories, plays, novels, and symbolic poetry. The works of Endre Ady, the most famous lyric poet of the twentieth century, brought out the beauty and power of the

Independent Picture Service

A portrait of Endre Ady depicts the poet sitting thoughtfully in a cafe. Many Hungarians consider Ady to be the country's greatest modern poet.

Hungarian language. Attila Jozsef used direct, simple, and witty language in his poems to describe the lives of Hungary's workers and common people. After the uprising of 1956, many writers fled the country to escape the government's restrictions on published works.

Ferenc Molnar enjoyed wide popularity outside Hungary in the early 1900s. One of his works, the play *Liliom*, became the basis of the Broadway musical *Carousel*. The tradition of theater remains strong throughout Hungary. More than a dozen theater companies perform regularly in Budapest. Many smaller cities and towns have at least one drama company.

Art and Music

Hungary's art flowered during the nineteenth century, a time when the nation was drawing closer to western Europe. Mihaly Munkacsi, the most famous Hungarian artist of the period, painted scenes of village life. Victor Madarasz and Bertalan Szekely created large, detailed paintings of episodes from Hungary's history.

As Hungarian artists traveled abroad to study, they absorbed new ideas about representing people and nature in their works. The French Impressionist style, in which artists freely interpret color and light, had a strong influence on nineteenth-century Hungarian artists, including Szinyei Merse. Mihaly Kosztka rendered vivid, dreamlike scenes from his own imagination. Margit Kovacs, Hungary's most famous ceramicist, used clay sculpture and reliefs to depict dreams and legends. An entire museum in the town of Szentendre is devoted to her works.

Hungary's classical music tradition dates to the use of chants in the early Christian churches. By the 1700s, many of

Dancers in traditional costume spin through a lively Hungarian folk dance.

Bela Bartok's musical innovations—many of them developed from Hungarian folk music—made him one of the most famous composers of the twentieth century.

the kingdom's wealthy families had private orchestras and composers. The Esterhazy family, for example, employed Joseph Haydn, an Austrian musician and one of the world's most famous classical composers.

The nineteenth-century composer Ferenc Erkel wrote popular songs, operas, and the Hungarian national anthem. Franz Liszt, a Hungarian-born pianist, thrilled audiences all over Europe with his fiery performances. Liszt and Erno Dohnanyi, another Hungarian composer, relied on the traditional harmonies used in western Europe to write their music.

Hungarian music moved in a new direction during the 1900s. Bela Bartok wove Hungarian folk melodies into his string quartets, piano pieces, and orchestral works. Bartok abandoned classical harmony to create a new musical style based on unusual chords and musical scales. Zoltan Kodaly, a close colleague of Bartok, also borrowed folk melodies but used traditional harmony in his works.

Folk musicians perform on violins and on a dulcimer, a traditional stringed instrument.

Pods of paprika dry in storage before being ground into a fine powder. Paprika is the most popular spice among Hungarian cooks.

The music of the Gypsies has had a strong effect on Hungarian folk music. Sad melodies and five-note scales characterize many Hungarian folk songs. The *kuruc* songs, which originated in Rakoczi's revolt of 1711, are still widely sung. Hungarian folk musicians favor clarinets, violins, and the dulcimer, a stringed instrument played with small mallets.

Food

The settlement of Hungary by Magyars, Germans, and people of the Balkan region has given the country a wide variety of foods. The most popular meats are pork, beef, and veal. Pork is also the main ingredient of many kinds of sausages and salamis. Meats are usually highly seasoned, with ground paprika or red pepper giving them characteristic spice. Hungarians serve chicken with paprika on festive occasions.

The country's best-known dish is goulash (*gulyas* in Hungarian), a thick stew of beef, onions, potatoes, and gravy seasoned with paprika. Main courses are accompanied by noodles, potatoes, or *galuska*, a Hungarian pasta.

Hungarians end their meals with sweet desserts, including strudel, a pastry with a thin crust and a filling of cheese or fruit. Adults enjoy wine with their evening meal. Tokaji wines from northeastern Hungary are known throughout Europe. Hungary also produces various brandies distilled with apricots, plums, and other fruits.

Recreation and Sports

Hungary provides many opportunities to enjoy outdoor sports. Hikers visit the mountains of the northeast, and sailors take advantage of the brisk winds on Lake Balaton. Recreational fishing is popular in the streams and rivers of Transdanubia. Hungarians relax at the country's health resorts, where underground mineral springs feed natural and artificial pools.

Football (soccer) is the most popular team sport in Hungary. Schools, factories, and large farms have set up their own soccer clubs, and Hungary has participated

A table is set with spice, peppers, bread, and stew during a Hungarian cookout.

Photo © William Weems

51

The Hungarian boxer Laszlo Papp *(center)* waits to receive his gold medal at the 1952 Summer Olympics in Helsinki, Finland.

in European and World Cup soccer championships. Hungarians also play basketball and volleyball. Hungary's young team of chess players, including the Polgar sisters and Ildiko Madi, defeated a strong Russian team in competition in 1988. Judit Polgar gained international renown after defeating the grandmaster Boris Spassky in 1993.

Hungarian athletes have excelled at the Olympic Games. The Hungarian team was awarded 30 medals at the 1992 Summer Olympics, including gold medals in wrestling, kayaking, fencing, women's gymnastics, and swimming.

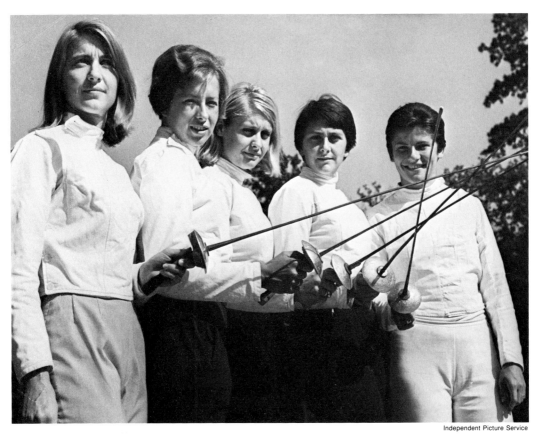

The Hungarian women's fencing team won a silver medal at the 1968 Summer Olympics in Mexico City.

In Decs, a village in southern Hungary, a woman weaves carpets on a wooden loom. Many small workshops that make traditional handicrafts still operate in rural Hungary.

4) The Economy

Before World War II, farming was the largest sector of the Hungarian economy. Although Hungarian companies operated mines and factories, these businesses produced a relatively small percentage of the nation's economic output.

After the war, the new Communist regime began an intensive program of industrialization. The government took over factories, mines, and other businesses and managed the economy. A series of five-year plans set production goals, wages, and prices. As part of the trading bloc of eastern European countries, Hungary took much of its direction from Soviet planners.

By the early 1960s, however, the government's poor management was causing the economy to decline. Production was falling, and many goods were in short supply. In response, Hungary's leader Janos Kadar allowed smaller, private companies to operate. The government relaxed its control over foreign trade. As a result,

A worker operates heavy equipment at a Hungarian steel plant. A vital part of the Hungarian economy, steelworks supply essential material for cars, heavy equipment, and building construction.

merchants could offer products that were scarce in other eastern European nations.

In 1968 Kadar's regime introduced the New Economic Mechanism (NEM). Under this program, the government set long-range goals but allowed factory managers to run day-to-day operations. The NEM lessened controls over wages and prices and permitted foreign companies to invest in Hungarian manufacturing firms.

By the 1980s, most state-owned businesses were setting their own wages, prices, and production goals. The number of private businesses and foreign partnerships was rising. Hungary managed to create a more open economy in which production, especially among smaller manufacturing businesses, slowly improved. By the early 1990s, after the fall of the Communists from power, Hungary was selling its state-owned businesses and was trading freely with western Europe.

Hungary still faces serious economic problems. The government borrowed extensively to pay for business improvements. The heavy burden of debt, as well as low prices for Hungary's products on the world market, has slowed growth. But the country's attempts at modernizing its economy may have sheltered it from the severe problems occurring in other ex-Communist European nations.

Manufacturing

Manufacturing in Hungary grew rapidly after World War II as the state took control of manufacturing businesses and built new factories. With a series of five-year plans, the government set out high production goals for steel, transportation equipment, and heavy machinery.

Many of Hungary's state-owned industries are now being sold. Factory managers are free to set wages and prices according to supply and demand. Yet Hungary still has trouble competing with companies in western Europe. A weak market for their products is forcing many manufacturers to scale back their operations or to go out of business.

Foreign investment has helped some Hungarian industries to expand. Businesses based in the United States have built car-parts factories and computer plants. Hungarian workers assemble cars for Japanese firms, and a Swiss company cooperates with Hungary in making medicines. Austrian and German firms are also investing in Hungarian manufacturing.

Plants in Budapest produce cars, buses, and railroad equipment. Steel and cement factories supply the construction industry.

Other important Hungarian goods include shoes, aluminum, engines, televisions, fertilizers, and textiles. Although most factories are located in Budapest and northern Hungary, companies have built new plants in the Nagyalfold and in Pecs. A modern industrial center has also been built in Dunaujvaros, a city 35 miles south of Budapest on the Danube.

Agriculture and Forestry

After coming to power, Hungary's Communist government seized cropland and organized collective farms. As collective workers, farmers became landless laborers who shared their work as well as the money earned from selling their crops. By the late 1980s, collectives covered more

Photo © William Weems

Horses troop through a pasture in rural Hungary. For centuries, the breeding of horses has been an important occupation on the plains of the Hortobagy region.

55

Shepherds gather their flock on a farm in the Hortobagy.

than two-thirds of the country's farmland. State-owned farms, which are directly managed by the government, now take up another 15 percent of the land. Private farmers hold only a small percentage.

The Communist regime strictly controlled prices for farm goods, although it spent little money on modernizing agriculture. This policy resulted in poor harvests and falling production. In the 1970s, as the government relaxed price controls, farm production began to rise. In the early 1990s, agriculture provided about 20 percent of the country's economic output and employed about 25 percent of the people.

Hungarian farms benefit from fertile soil and a mild climate. More than half of the country's land is used for pasture or crop growing. Irrigation projects have brought water to areas of the Nagyalfold that receive little rainfall. In addition, the draining of marshes in the Danube valley has created new cropland. Modern fertilizers and machinery have increased yields,

Harvesting machines cross a field of wheat on the Hungarian plain. Fertile land and a moderate climate have helped Hungarian farmers to produce a surplus of food crops.

Once performed by hand, onion picking has been mechanized in Hungary. The faster machines have allowed farmers to increase their yields of this important crop.

enabling Hungary to export food to other European countries.

The Nagyalfold supports cereal crops, including wheat, rye, and barley. Farmers also breed cattle and horses on the open plains. Potatoes, corn, and sugar beets are important crops in the rest of the nation. On pastures and in the highlands, Hungarian farmers raise cattle, pigs, sheep, and poultry for products such as milk, meat, butter, eggs, and wool.

Agriculture students help to gather a crop of Riesling grapes, which will be processed into white wine.

Farmers plant rice in the Tisza valley, grow paprika near the city of Szeged, and raise tobacco in the northwest. Cereal grains, potatoes, and cattle are major products of the Kisalfold. Wines from the Tokaj region are famous throughout Europe, and vineyards thrive near Pecs and north of Lake Balaton.

To create farmland, Hungarians cut down many of the country's forests, which once covered a large part of Transdanubia and the highlands of the northeast. A reforestation program has replaced some lost woodlands, but Hungarian forests are unable to meet the demand for timber. As a result, the country must import wood from foreign suppliers for construction and papermaking.

Mining and Energy

Hungarian mines were once among the most productive in eastern Europe. Although the country still produces minerals and energy fuels, output has declined as mines have been exhausted. The Mecsek Mountains of the southeast contain coal as well as uranium ore, which can be refined to generate nuclear power. Deposits of bauxite exist in the Bakony Forest and in the highlands north of Lake Balaton.

Hungary has small oil deposits southwest of Lake Balaton, and natural gas in the Nagyalfold. During the 1980s, pipelines carrying natural gas and oil from the Soviet Union supplied half of Hungary's energy needs. In the early 1990s, the

Photo © William Weems

A huge crane scrapes a hillside for mineral ore. Although many of the country's mineral deposits have been exhausted, Hungary still produces coal, bauxite, and uranium.

A tram winds through the streets of Budapest. As an important producer of transportation equipment in Europe, Hungary benefited from its own manufacturing expertise to create an efficient public transportation system.

republics that had made up the Soviet Union declared their independence. As a result, imports of oil and natural gas to Europe declined. Hungary must now make up the shortage by buying more expensive fuels from the Middle East.

Transportation and Tourism

The Danube River, which flows south through central Hungary, has long been one of the most important trading routes in Europe. Seagoing ships use the river to travel between the busy port of Budapest and the Black Sea, where the Danube ends. A network of canals links the Danube with other regions of Hungary.

The country's road network includes 20,000 miles of paved and unpaved routes. The state-owned railway uses 5,600 miles of track, linking the country's major cities as well as smaller towns. Hungary's road

Automobiles, buses, and trams share Budapest's downtown streets, where local businesses use many of the city's buildings as billboards.

Independent Picture Service

Hikers enjoy a pleasant view in hilly Transdanubia.

and rail connections to Austria allow it to transport goods easily to the rest of western Europe. Malev, the Hungarian airline, flies to foreign cities from Ferihegy, an international airport near Budapest.

As one of the first eastern European nations to freely open its borders to visitors, Hungary has a well-developed tourist industry. Luxury hotels in Budapest accommodate travelers who visit the capital's churches, museums, and historic sites. The government has also built campsites to attract hikers to Hungary's forests and mountainous areas. Spas, mineral baths, and health resorts exist throughout the country. Tourists also flock to the shores of Lake Balaton for sailing, swimming, and sunbathing.

The tourism industry brings in about $2 billion in foreign exchange every year. Most visitors to Hungary arrive from central European countries, including Austria, the Czech Republic, and Slovakia.

Independent Picture Service

Fertod Palace, the home of the noble Esterhazy family, is one of Hungary's most popular tourist attractions. Beginning in 1761, the Esterhazy princes employed the Austrian composer Joseph Haydn as their musical director.

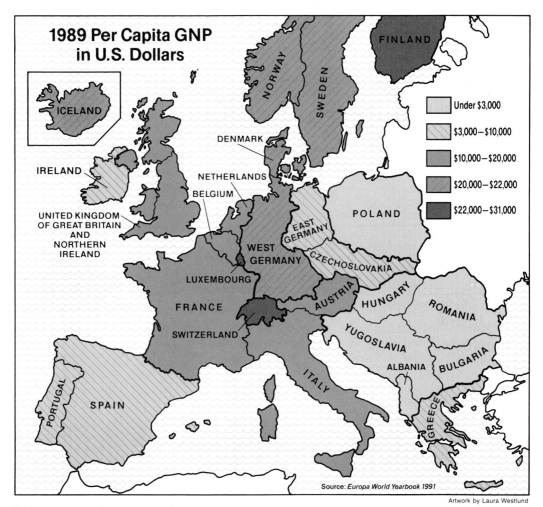

1989 Per Capita GNP in U.S. Dollars

Under $3,000

$3,000–$10,000

$10,000–$20,000

$20,000–$22,000

$22,000–$31,000

ICELAND

NORWAY

SWEDEN

FINLAND

DENMARK

IRELAND

NETHERLANDS

BELGIUM

UNITED KINGDOM OF GREAT BRITAIN AND NORTHERN IRELAND

EAST GERMANY

POLAND

WEST GERMANY

CZECHOSLOVAKIA

LUXEMBOURG

AUSTRIA

HUNGARY

ROMANIA

FRANCE

SWITZERLAND

YUGOSLAVIA

ALBANIA

BULGARIA

PORTUGAL

SPAIN

ITALY

GREECE

Source: *Europa World Yearbook 1991*

Artwork by Laura Westlund

This map compares the average wealth per person—calculated by gross national product (GNP) per capita—for 26 European countries. The GNP is the value of all goods and services produced by a country in a year. To arrive at the GNP per capita, each nation's total GNP is divided by its population figure. Hungary's 1989 figure of $2,560 was one of the highest GNP rates among the former Communist nations of central and eastern Europe. The Hungarian GNP increased in the early 1990s as the country's newly privatized firms increased their production.

Foreign Trade

For 40 years, the Soviet Union and its allies in eastern Europe were Hungary's most important trading partners. During the 1980s, Hungary's government expanded trade and banking connections to western Europe. Hungary also encouraged joint ventures, in which foreign businesses form partnerships with Hungarian companies. These policies allowed Hungary to expand its foreign trade, which brought in money needed for economic development.

Hungary now has a trade surplus, meaning the country earns more money from its exports than it spends on its imports.

Hungary sells medicines, machinery, transportation equipment, chemicals, and steel to foreign buyers. Agricultural products—including food, livestock, and wine—make up one-third of the country's total exports. To meet its energy needs, Hungary imports coal and petroleum. Iron ore, chemicals, machinery, and cotton are also imported.

61

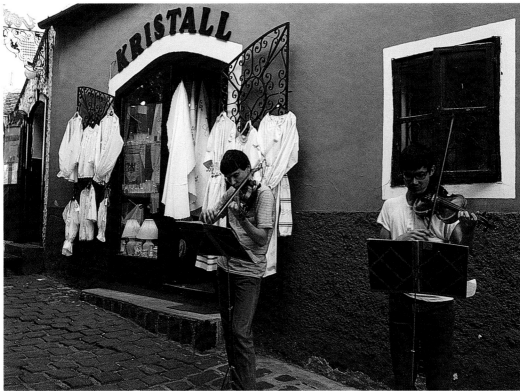

Musicians perform outside a clothing store in Szentendre.

Hungary's largest trading partners are Germany, Austria, and Italy. The government has also made an agreement with the European Community (EC), an association of western European nations. The agreement is meant to expand trade between Hungary and the EC countries.

The Future

Unlike many eastern European countries, Hungary experienced a peaceful transition from Communism to a democratic system. Because the government had already loosened its control of production, prices, and wages, the country was prepared for economic changes. Hungary has established successful trade relations with other European nations and will eventually benefit from a more open European market.

A horseman rests during an outdoor festival on the *puszta*, or plains, of eastern Hungary. Tourists enjoy the colorful costumes worn by Hungarian riders.

Yet Hungary still must overcome serious problems caused by the difficult transition from a planned to a free-market economy. For example, industrial production is falling as firms that are losing money go out of business. Unemployment and prices are rising, making goods less affordable for Hungarian consumers. In addition, the Communist regime borrowed large amounts of money to modernize industry, and this burden of foreign debt is slowing new investment. Hungarians are seeing their incomes decline while the government reduces its support for unemployment, health, and social-security benefits.

Hungary's future depends on the success and stability of the rest of eastern Europe. Conflict in the former Yugoslavia is causing turmoil on Hungary's southern border, and Ukraine and Romania are suffering economic decline. Although Hungary is making some progress, it will benefit greatly if its former partners in the Communist bloc can peacefully develop their own economies.

Women carefully paint designs on glazed ceramic pieces in a small workshop. Many Hungarians are still employed in making traditional pottery, clothes, carpets, and tableware.

Photo © William Weems

63

Index

Academy of Sciences, 32
Ady, Endre, 48
Agriculture, 14-15, 19, 53, 55-58
Alps, 11
Angevin dynasty, 26-27
Antall, Jozsef, 41
Aquincum, 17, 22
Architecture, 16, 18
Arpad, 23-25, 39
Arpad dynasty, 24-26, 44
Art, 48-49
Asia Minor, 7, 27
Austria, 8, 10-11, 30, 34-35, 60, 62
Austria-Hungary, 34-35
Avars, 22
Bakony Forest, 11, 58
Bakony Mountains, 11
Balaton, Lake, 11, 13, 15, 20-21, 51, 58, 60
Balkan Peninsula, 27, 37
Bartok, Bela, 49
Bavaria, 24
Bela IV, 26
Bethlen, Gabor, 30
Bibliotheca Corvina, 28
Black Sea, 59
Borzsony Hills, 11
Bosnia, 35
Britain, 35, 37
Buda, 17, 19, 29-30, 32, 34
Budapest, 7, 8, 11-13, 16-19, 22, 25, 35-39, 43-47, 55, 59-60
Bukk Mountains, 11
Carpathian Mountains, 11, 13, 23, 26
Charlemagne, 22
Charles Robert (Charles I), 26
Christianity, 7, 19, 23-24, 44
Cities, 16-20. See also Budapest; Debrecen; Miskolc; Szeged
Climate, 13-14
Communists, 8, 18, 35-41, 45-47, 55-56, 62-63
Constitutions, 34, 38, 40-42
Corvinus, Matthias, 17, 28-29
Council of Ministers, 42
Croatia, 10, 25, 43
Croatians, 34, 44
Cumania, 11, 14
Czechoslovakia, 10, 35-37
Danube River, 10, 11-14, 16-17, 21-22, 59
Danube River Valley, 12, 14-15, 21-22, 29, 56
Debrecen, 19, 37, 44, 46
Dohnanyi, Erno, 49
Dunaujvaros, 55
Eastern Canal, 13
Eastern Orthodox Church, 45
Economy, 9, 34, 36-37, 39, 53-63
Education, 19, 34, 46
Endre (Andras) II, 26
Energy, 16, 58-59, 61
Eotvos Lorant University, 19
Esztergom, 3, 11, 24
Ethnic heritage, 7, 34, 43-44
Europe, 7-12, 19, 22, 24-25, 27, 36, 41, 54, 61
European Community, 41, 62
Fauna, 14-15
Ferenc Rakoczi II, 31
Ferihegy, 60
Fertod Palace, 60
Flag, 39

Flora, 14
Food, 8, 15, 50-51
Foreign investment, 40-41, 54-55, 61
Forests, 14, 58
France, 23, 26, 35, 37
Franks, 22-23
Franz Joseph, 33-34
Future outlook, 62-63
General Workers party, 34
Germans, 7-8, 23, 34, 44-45, 50
Germany, 23-24, 30-31, 35, 37, 45, 62
Geza, 24
Golden Bull (charter), 26
Gombos, Gyula, 37
Goncz, Arpad, 41
Government, 8-9, 13, 41-42, 62-63
Great Church, The, 19
Grosz, Karoly, 40
Gypsies, 44, 50
Habsburg Empire, 7-8, 16, 19, 29-35, 48
Haydn, Joseph, 49, 60
Health, 47
History, 7-8, 17-18, 21-42
   Communism, 35-36, 38-41
   democracy, 8, 40-42, 62
   Habsburg Empire, 7-8, 16, 19, 29-35, 48
   Magyars, 7, 9, 23-27, 43, 50
   Ottoman Empire, 27-30
   Roman rule, 21-23
   world wars, 35-38
Hitler, Adolf, 37
Horthy, Miklos, 36
Hortobagy, 11-12, 55-56
Hungarian Democratic Forum, 41
Hungary, Republic of, 7-10, 39, 43, 62-63
   boundaries, size, and location of, 10
   flag of, 39
   future outlook of, 62-63
   population of, 43
Hunyadi, Janos, 28
Illyrians, 21-22
Independence party, 35
Industry, 18-20, 34, 37, 40, 53-55, 63
Infant mortality, 47
Israel, 45
Italy, 23, 35, 37, 62
Jews, 45
Joseph II, 32
Jozsef, Attila, 48
Judicial system, 42
Kadar, Janos, 39-40, 53-54
Karolyi, Mihaly, 35
Kekes, Mount, 11
Khrushchev, Nikita, 38
Kisalfold (Little Plain), 11, 13, 58
Kiskore Reservoir, 12
Kodaly, Zoltan, 49
Komarom, 47
Korishegy, Mount, 11
Koros River, 13
Kossuth, Lajos, 19, 32-34
Kossuth University, 20
Kovacs, Margit, 49
Kun, Bela, 35-36
Lajos I, 26-27
Lajos II, 29
Land, 10-20
Language, 43-44, 46, 48

Laszlo I, 25
Laszlo II, 29
Life expectancy, 47
Liszt, Franz, 49
Literacy, 46
Livestock, 19, 56-57
Lutheran Church, 45
Magyars, 7, 9, 23-25, 43, 50
Manufacturing, 18-19, 40, 54-55
Maps, 6, 15, 25, 35, 61
Maria Theresa, 31-32
Matra Mountains, 11, 16
Mecsek Mountains, 11, 16, 58
Minerals, 15, 29, 58
Mining, 15-16, 26, 58
Miskolc, 19-20, 23
Mongols, 26
Music and dance, 4, 9, 20, 49-50
Nagy, Imre, 38-40, 42
Nagyalfold (Great Plain), 10-13, 16, 22-23, 29, 55-58
National Assembly, 40-42
Natural resources, 15-16
Nemeth, Miklos, 40
New Economic Mechanism (NEM), 39, 54
Olympic Games, 9, 52
Otto I, 24
Ottoman Empire, 27-30
Ottoman Turks, 7-8, 17, 23, 27-30
Pannonia, 22-23
Paprika, 8, 20, 50-51, 58
People, 43-52
   education, 19, 34, 46
   ethnic heritage, 7, 34, 43-44
   literacy, 46
   population, 43
Pest, 17, 26, 33-34
Petofi, Alexander (Sandor), 33, 48
Pilis Hills, 11
Poland, 30, 37, 45
Polgar, Judit, 52
Protestant Reformation, 19, 30-32, 44
Prussia, 31
Raba River, 13
Railways, 34, 59-60
Rainfall, 13
Rakosi, Matyas, 38
Recreation, 51, 60
Reforestation, 14, 58
Reformed Church, 44
Religion, 7, 19, 30, 44-45
Rivers, 12-13. See also Danube River
Roads, 59-60
Roman Catholic Church, 24, 30
Roman Empire, 21-23
Romania, 10, 36, 44, 63
Royal Palace, 18-19
Russia, 33-36. See also Soviet Union
Serbia, 10, 12, 43
Serbs, 34, 44-45
Sigismund, 27-28
Slovakia, 10, 12, 43, 47, 60
Slovaks, 34, 44
Slovenes, 44
Slovenia, 10
Socialists, 35, 41
Sopron, 7, 16
Soviet Union, 8, 17-18, 35-41, 46, 53, 58-59, 61
Sports, 9, 51-52
Standard of living, 39, 61

Stephen (Istvan) I, 23-24, 39, 44
Szechenyi, Istvan, 32-33
Szeged, 20, 46, 58
Szentendre, 14, 45, 62
Tac, 21
Theater, 48
Thirty Years' War, 30
Tiberius, 22
Tisza, Kalman, 34
Tisza River, 12-14, 16, 20
Topography, 10-11
Tourism, 60, 62
Trade, 9, 12, 26, 29, 53-54, 61-62
Transdanubia, 11, 14, 16, 20-21, 51, 58, 60
Transdanubian Central Highlands, 11
Transportation, 5, 12-13, 18, 29, 34, 59-60
Transylvania, 25-26, 28-31, 33, 36, 44
Treaty of Trianon, 36-37
Turkey, 35
Ukraine, 10, 63
Unemployment, 36, 40, 63
Urbanization, 14, 16, 43
Vac, 12
Veszprem, 20
World War I, 8, 35-36
World War II, 8, 17, 19, 23, 37-38, 45-46, 53-54
Yugoslavia, 10, 35-36, 44, 63
Zala River, 13